OCEANS OF LOVE

By Katherine Harms

A month of meditations on the boundless love of God

Copyright © 2008 by Katherine Harms
All rights reserved

Edited and revised © 2016 by Katherine Harms
All rights reserved

Scripture quotations are taken from the following sources:
NRSV The Holy Bible: New Revised Standard Version. Nashville: Thomas Nelson Publishers, 1989

MSG Scripture taken from THE MESSAGE copyright 1993, 1994, 1995, 1996, 2000, 2001, 2002. Used by permission of NavPress Publishing Group.

NIV84 Scripture taken from HOLY BIBLE, NEW INTERNATIONAL VERSION. Copyright 1973, 1978, 1984 by International Bible Society. Used by permission of Zondervan Publishing House.

AB Scripture quotations taken from the Amplified Bible, Copyright 1954, 1958, 1962, 1964, 1965, 1987 by The Lockman Foundation. Used by permission.

NET Scripture quoted by permission. Quotations designated (NET) are from The NET Bible® Copyright © 2005 by Biblical Studies Press, L.L.C. www.netbible.com All rights reserved.

ISBN-13: 978-1532994838

ISBN-10: 1532994834

Printed by CreateSpace, an Amazon.com Company

Available from Amazon.com and other retail outlets

Contents

INTRODUCTION V

DAY 1 1

DAY 2 2

DAY 3 4

DAY 4 6

DAY 5 8

DAY 6 9

DAY 7 11

DAY 8 14

DAY 9 16

DAY 10 18

DAY 11 21

DAY 12 23

DAY 13 25

DAY 14 27

DAY 15 29

DAY 16	31
DAY 17	33
DAY 18	35
DAY 19	39
DAY 20	41
DAY 21	43
DAY 22	44
DAY 23	46
DAY 24	48
DAY 25	50
DAY 26	53
DAY 27	55
DAY 28	58
DAY 29	61
DAY 30	63
DAY 31	65
AFTERWORD	68
NOTES	69

Introduction

People who live on boats are not known for their spirituality. I, however, can testify that my years of living on a boat and traveling over the ocean have opened my eyes to God's presence with me on his great oceans. Because our boat (S/V No Boundaries) is only 45 feet long and not quite 14 feet wide, it is a challenge to find private space for the purpose of meditation, Bible study, or prayer. Yet the experience of navigating and living on the ocean has powerfully motivated me to make time for God.

I most often make my personal space in the forward cabin. When sailing conditions permit, I love to go forward of the mast on deck where all I can really hear is the wind and the song of the rigging. Spending time each day in such a place is a good way to nourish and maintain a life of faith while cruising on a sailboat. The concept works equally well under a tree in an RV campground, in the spare bedroom at home, or on a rock at the edge of a creek. The discipline of private meditation and prayer is wholesome and nourishing in any way of life.

The purpose of this book is to encourage prayerful consideration of some biblical texts whose superficial link is a reference to oceans or water. The Bible uses references to familiar things to teach us about unfamiliar things. The selected texts use our experience with oceans and water to teach us about our relationship with God. The Bible records that God yearns for a relationship with each of us. These texts show both God's fervent desire for relationship with us and many ways that we can respond to his call.

I encourage each reader to make time daily to allow the Holy Spirit, God's own breath, to transform and empower a life energized by God's overwhelming, saving love.

Please write to me at katherine@katherineharms.com and let me know if this book has been valuable to you or if you see opportunities for improvement.

Katherine Harms
Aboard the sailing vessel *No Boundaries*

Day 1

> God spoke:
> "Separate!
> Water-beneath-Heaven, gather into one place;
> Land, appear!"
> And there it was.
> God named the land Earth.
> He named the pooled water Ocean.
> God saw that it was good.
>
> Genesis 1:9-10 MSG

God speaks. Light! Sky! Then the oceans and dry land appear. What God says, happens. When I speak, things don't always happen, or if things happen, they may be quite different from my intention. When God speaks, the word takes on physical existence. Clearly, God is not like us.

Ocean was created on the third day. Photos from space show us that ocean is still the dominant feature of creation. When we sail the oceans we leave sight of land, and far at sea we might think we had returned to the moment just after God said, "Sky!" We see sky above, but all around is only water, just as it might have been before land could be seen.

The ocean is a primeval force, unchanged in its power and mystery after 4 billion years. The duration of 4 billion years and the awesome mass of the sea make us feel insignificant. That feeling is wrong. We are very significant. God did not stop at creating oceans. He created all the earth and all the creatures, and when everything was ready, he created people. Like a mother preparing for a baby, he prepared for us. After we were created, he walked with us to help us grow up. When we believed a lie and broke the relationship, as any mother would do, he came for us himself. He spoke the word "Love," and then he brought love to life by dying. When we feel insignificant in the vastness of the ocean, or in the bedroom at home, or in the cubicle at work, or wherever we may be, we must remember that God came for us. He values us. Human beings count to the God whose words live.

Day 2

> As long as the earth endures,
> seedtime and harvest, cold and heat,
> summer and winter, day and night,
> shall not cease.
>
> Genesis 8:22 NRSV

> This is what the Lord says, he who appoints the sun to shine by day, who decrees the moon and stars to shine by night, who stirs up the sea so that its waves roar—the Lord Almighty is his name: "Only if these decrees vanish from my sight," declares the Lord, "will the descendants of Israel ever cease to be a nation before me."
>
> Jeremiah 31:35-36 NIV

The immutable laws of nature speak of God's unchanging love for people. He says very clearly that if the order of nature could be ended, then, and only then, could he forget his children. What a powerful and comforting truth. If the God who stirs up hurricanes could lose his power, then, and only then, he could quit loving us.

In the far corners of the earth, in the midst of the great sea, in the silence of a hidden cove, in the heart of a terrible storm – no matter what nature throws at us, its obedience to the natural laws is a reminder that God has not forgotten us. If the laws of nature are still working, then God still loves us. We should never ask for them not to work, because God has given them as a sign of his love.

Things do happen that make us wonder if God knows. When our hearts are broken by poisoned relationships, when disasters of wind and wave overwhelm our ability to cope, it is tempting to ask God to step in and change the laws of nature. When we are at the mercy of these laws, because they are working exactly the way they have always worked, we yearn for some magic word that will change everything. We want power to change the natural laws, because the natural consequences of those laws hurt us. However, that is not God's plan. He promises us that as long as we can count on those laws to work, we can also count on him.

People are important to God. He loves people, his supreme creation. He wants us to be able to believe in him, and this promise shines light into our dark nights. In the book of Psalms, there are many statements invoking praise from nature. "The heavens declare the glory of God" (Psalm 19:1 NIV). The mountains "skip like rams" (Psalm 114:6 NRSV). "Praise him sun and moon, praise him all you shining stars" (Psalm 148:3 NRSV). The apostle Paul even said, "Ever since the creation of the world [God's] eternal power and divine nature, invisible though they are, have been understood and seen through the things he has made" (Romans 1:20 NRSV).

It sounds paradoxical to say that when we are most captive to the laws of nature, we should be most deeply confirmed in our faith, but then everything about God looks paradoxical when compared to the teachings Satan has promoted in the world at large. The next time you are captive to a Force 8 wind, remember that your God loves you. You have great value to God. You can count on it.

Day 3

> For I am the Lord your God,
> who stirs up the sea so that its waves roar—
> the Lord of hosts is his name.
>
> Isaiah 51:15 NRSV

It is dark. It feels as if it has been a week since sundown. The sea is in tumult, and the boat is struggling to find its way. You are asking yourself what possessed you to think that this adventure was worth everything. You know exactly what Isaiah meant about waves that roar.

Isaiah's words were written to people who were imprisoned and exiled from their homes. The king who defeated their homeland in battle had moved them to a foreign place where they had been living in exile more than fifty years. They kept telling each other the stories of God's miraculous signs and wonders when he brought Israel out of Egypt, but they were starting to fear that God didn't care anymore.

It happens to everyone. Present troubles make us look back with nostalgia for the "good old days." We wonder what went wrong that put us in the midst of difficulties. When a storm at sea appears, seemingly out of nowhere, it is tempting to doubt our ability to survive it. Waves that look like mountains make us feel the way the Israelites felt when faced with the implacable power of the Babylonian empire. We are overwhelmed.

God reminds us in these verses that he is the one who can stir up the giant waves. We know what it takes to do that. When the largest boat ever built travels through the ocean, its wake doesn't even begin to demonstrate the power of a storm wave. The turbulence of a big ship is powerful, but no boat can set off the wave action of a hurricane.

The God who can do this cares about us. Whether we face mortal men bent on hurting us or impersonal wind and wave, God cares for us. Our lives matter to him.

God says in these verses that his power is greater than any power that threatens us. His power can move the waves. His power breaks apart the rocks in the bowels of the earth. When his power reaches out to rescue us, we shall be rescued. He will not fail.

No matter what challenges we face, and no matter how tough it seems for us to face our challenges, these verses remind us that God never lets go of us. The God who stirs the rage of the sea is with us through that rage. We can trust him with our lives.

> For he knows how we were made; he remembers that we are dust.
>
> Psalm 103:14 NRSV

Day 4

> Jonah immediately headed off to Tarshish to escape from the commission of the Lord.... So he paid the fare and went aboard it to go with them to Tarshish far away from the Lord. But the Lord hurled a powerful wind on the sea. Such a violent tempest arose on the sea that the ship threatened to break up!
>
> Jonah 1:3-4 NET

God came down to Jonah and gave him a job. Moreover, God asked Jonah to do something repugnant. He does that with all his children sooner or later. "Love your neighbor" can be a repugnant task if your neighbor has anchored his boat carelessly, and you know that you will need to stay up all night to protect your own boat. God asked Jonah to do something loving for people he detested; God wanted Jonah to bring the message of salvation to Nineveh. Imagine if you had a house in a nice suburban neighborhood and a gang moved in next door to manufacture and sell meth. Your first instinct probably would not be to knock on the door and say, "God loves you."

Yet this is the message God gave to Jonah. Oh, it sounds at first glance like a very negative message: "Announce judgment against [Nineveh's] people because their wickedness has come to my attention" (Jonah 1:2 NET). However, if you read the story to the end, you learn that when the people repented, God forgave them and spared their city. It was always in his mind to save them from destruction. That is why he sent Jonah, and that is why Jonah did not want to go. Jonah preferred that Nineveh be destroyed. Nineveh was the enemy, and he did not love the people of Nineveh. Jonah was not ready to love that neighbor.

When God sent a terrible storm to engulf the boat on which Jonah tried to run away, he gave Jonah two clear messages. First, he really did want Jonah to be the one who delivered the message. God loved Jonah, and God wanted Jonah to learn how to love people the way God loved them. Second, he really did want Nineveh to repent and be spared from judgment and destruction. God took extraordinary measures such as the violent storm, because he loves people. He loved Jonah, and he loved the people of Nineveh.

When we see the lengths to which God extended himself for these people, it should increase our faith that God loves us, too. Even if we are disobedient. Even if we are wicked. Even if we have gone a long way in the wrong direction. People are important to God. Adam and Eve were treasured, Abraham had immense value, Jonah was cherished, and you are beloved. You cannot run far enough to escape this love.

Day 5

> [Roaring] deep calls to [roaring] deep at the thunder of your waterspouts; all your breakers and your rolling waves have gone over me. Yet the Lord will command His loving-kindness in the daytime, and in the night His song shall be with me, a prayer to the God of my life.
>
> Psalm 42:7-8 AB

After three days in a row when the boat never comes to rest anywhere, when green water rolls over the bow and waves like mountains tower on every side, then we can imagine how it would feel to be abandoned by God. Out here, there is nobody who can help. If another boat does come along, the best we could hope for is to share our misery.

Even people who have never been to sea sometimes feel this way. The Psalmist dropped down to the bottom and felt overwhelmed, abandoned. He might have done a 360 rollover. But he did not give up. He professed his faith in the midst of all this violence, and his faith buoyed him like a lifejacket with neck support. Circumstance assaulted him and challenged his faith. The situation asked, "Does God care?" His faith answered, "The Lord will command his loving-kindness in the daytime, and in the night his song shall be with me" (Psalm 42:8 AB).

Each of us has known times when it seemed that everything and everyone was against us. Like the Psalmist, we feel wounded and battered. Our souls are "cast down" and "disquieted." We feel as if we are wandering in a dark, empty place where there is no one to help, no way to understand what is happening.

This is precisely the time to assert our faith. Like the Psalmist, threatened by satanic circumstances, we can say, "Hope in God." Like Jesus, face to face with Satan, we can say, "Worship the Lord your God, and serve only him." Just as working muscles against heavy resistance increases muscular strength, we can only grow our faith by exercising it. Even though the Psalmist felt so discouraged that he turned to God and asked, "Why have you forgotten me?" (Psalm 42:9 AB) he nevertheless declares, "I shall again praise him, my help and my God" (Psalm 42:11 NRSV). The Psalmist points the way for us to follow.

Day 6

> Get to work! For I am with you.' The God-of-the-Angel-Armies is speaking! 'Put into action the word I covenanted with you when you left Egypt. I'm living and breathing among you right now. Don't be timid. Don't hold back.'
>
> Haggai 2:4-5 MSG

Often when God is about to make an announcement or give someone a task, he, or his angel, says the words, "Don't be afraid." Or in this translation, "Don't be timid." These words remind us that God knows we are weak and frail created beings whom he can crush with a word. God knows we are dust. Nevertheless, we are dust that matters to him. Therefore, he comes to us with work for us to do, and he tells us not to be afraid, even though this work may look like an impossible mission.

When God gives us work to do, he also asks for commitment. He doesn't come to us with a survey to find out what we want. He doesn't suggest that the work will be easy, or that someone else will pick up wherever we leave off. In this text, he is giving people the job of rebuilding his temple, a daunting task without the engineers or the finances Solomon had brought to the work of the original temple. At other times he sent individuals into foreign countries to speak terrible words of judgment for which they were at risk of execution. After Jesus rose from the dead, he sent a few men and women away from the mount of ascension with instructions to tell his story to the whole world, even though he himself had suffered crucifixion for telling it. Over and over, God asks people to commit to do what appears to be impossible.

In God's upside down economy, this is how it works. In the world at large, we expect people to have a budget and a project plan before they get a mandate to do the job. God gives us the mandate, and then says, "Don't be afraid. I am with you." He expects us to trust him for the resources we need. He tells us not to hold back, because he is not going to hold back.

It sounds crazy, but it really works. Here's why. We do not work in our own strength. The God who can shake the heavens, the earth and the seas strengthens us. He is the one who commands and then empowers us. When God speaks, what he says, happens. We can rely on the God who said "Light!" and there was light.

Some people might doubt that God would ask anyone to set out to sea in a small boat and explore his creation. That mission is no wilder than some recorded in the Bible. How crazy did it look when Noah was building a giant boat on a dry plain? When Abraham took off for parts unknown with his whole family and all his livestock? When Moses left his family and a comfortable life to set out for Egypt? When God gives us a vision or a dream, we can't know the outcome, any more than Noah, or Abraham, or Moses knew. We only know that this is God's way. We are to walk in it. Moreover, always, always, as we are commissioned, he says, "Don't be afraid. I am with you." We are important to God.

Day 7

> When the waters saw you, O God,
> when the waters saw you, they were afraid;
> the very deep trembled.
> The clouds poured out water;
> the skies thundered;
> ...
> Your way was through the sea,
> your path, through the mighty waters;
> yet your footprints were unseen.
>
> Psalm 77:16-19 NRSV

I have seen storms on both oceans and inland waterways. I have watched a wall of water march inexorably toward our ship as we hurriedly prepared for the invisible hammer that would strike us even before the visible wall reached our boat. I have wandered from one place to another in the midst of storm, rain and wind, looking hopelessly for a place where the anchor could get a grip on the bottom. Black clouds have poured out their water, lightning's arrows have flashed on every side, ferocious wind has roared in my ears while I trembled, and I have looked for the path of the Lord through the mighty waters.

I think I know how the disciples felt when they set out to cross the Sea of Galilee with Jesus asleep in the boat.

> A windstorm arose on the sea, so great that the boat was being swamped by the waves; but he was asleep. And they went and woke him up, saying, "Lord, save us! We are perishing!" Matthew 8:24-25 NRSV

At first it seems a bit strange that the experienced fishermen called out to the carpenter newly-turned rabbi to save them in a storm. After all, it was unlikely that this is the first storm they had seen on the Sea of Galilee. It has a history, like most inland bodies of water, of rapidly-developing storms with steep, tight wave trains that would easily swamp a small boat. You would expect them to be prepared, even expecting this storm, and ready with strategies for survival.

Apparently this storm overwhelmed their experience. Desperate, they turned to Jesus. They cried out, "Lord, save us!" They had seen him perform miracles. He healed people near him and he healed people he could not even see. The disciples had just seen Jesus multiply five loaves of bread and two fish to feed five thousand people. Maybe he could do something miraculous to help them survive the storm. It is hard to imagine what they really expected – a suggestion for another reef? A course correction off the wind? Or the gift of increased strength to pull the boat into the wind and actually heave to?

They called to Jesus in desperation, but they were shocked by his response.

First, Jesus turned to the disciples and rebuked them. "Why are you such cowards, such faint-hearts?" (Matthew 8:26 MSG)

Was he making fun of their fear? They all knew men who went out to fish on this sea and did not return. Did he not understand the gravity of the situation? If I had been aboard, I am sure that I would be stunned to think that some landlubber would look around at this maelstrom and accuse me of being a coward. Where exactly did he get his nerve?

Then Jesus turned his face to the storm and said "Silence." The lexical notes on the Greek words used here say that there is an implied threat in the word Jesus used, a suggestion that if the storm failed to silence itself, Jesus would muzzle it. Any way you read the text, Jesus took authority over the storm, and it immediately stopped. Suddenly they were in a dead calm. A storm arose, Jesus spoke, and calm ensued.

Then the disciples were really amazed. We can't guess what they expected, but it is obvious that they never expected he could simply shut down the storm. I wonder how often the disciples recalled this incident in the tumultuous days of persecution in Jerusalem and other places after Pentecost. Did the memory of this experience give them the courage to hang on through those new storms?

A miracle makes a point. It is not small talk. It is an attention-getter, a sign, a wonder. On the Sea of Galilee Jesus spoke to nature and it behaved as an obedient child. The disciples never forgot. Jesus had made his point that he was one with the Creator. When he spoke, what he said, happened. Jesus said "Silence!" There was silence.

We can trust a God with this kind of power over nature. We can count on the God who made the laws of nature. We can believe that He is able to comfort us and deliver us from all the challenges that come our way. Because He is God.

From Whirlwind came your thundering voice,
Lightning exposed the world,
Earth reeled and rocked.
You strode right through Ocean,
walked straight through roaring Ocean,
but nobody saw you come or go.

   Psalm 77:16-19 MSG

Day 8

> You cast me into the deep,
> into the heart of the seas,
> and the flood surrounded me;
> all your waves and your billows
> passed over me.
>
> Jonah 2:3-4 NRSV

God instructed Jonah to "arise and go" to Nineveh and Jonah chose to "arise and flee" to Tarshish. Tell a teenager to clean his room and you may soon discover that the one who is too tired to do the cleaning is plenty energetic to be out and about doing something else. God landed on Jonah as any good parent lands on a disobedient child. After a near-death experience, from the belly of a great fish, Jonah acknowledged that God had a right to be upset with him. He confessed that when the sailors threw him overboard to save themselves, he thought he was going to die.

God was not pleased with Jonah's decisions, but God did not give up on Jonah. The fact that Jonah could pray this prayer from the "safety" of the fish's belly demonstrates that God wasn't finished with Jonah yet. Even though Jonah had behaved despicably, God wanted a relationship with him. This story is one of many in the Bible which describe the lengths to which God will go in order to build relationships with people. It should be encouraging to each of us to know that God doesn't just throw up his hands in despair when we mess up. If he did, no one would have any hope. Like a mother grabbing her toddler by the collar and reining him in, God grabbed Jonah and gave him a timeout inside the fish. There, Jonah came to understand his experience and to recognize that "Deliverance belongs to the Lord" (Psalm 3:8 NRSV).

As a result of this experience two good things happened. First, Jonah went to Nineveh as instructed, and due to his obedience in delivering God's message, the people of Nineveh repented of their sins. Second, even though Jonah resented the fact that God didn't destroy the people, he came to understand that as God had delivered him, God also wanted to deliver the people of Nineveh. Jonah learned that God prefers to save people rather than to destroy them. He learned that God wants a relationship with people.

We can take comfort in this truth. When God seems as far away from us as Jonah thought he was in the depths of the sea, we can recall how God reached out and rescued first Jonah and then the whole city of Nineveh. God loved and salvaged these very disobedient and rebellious people. He will do the same for us.

Day 9

> Jesus came toward them walking on the water.
>
> Matthew 14:22 MSG

If ever the disciples had ever wondered who Jesus was, seeing him walk on water should have answered their questions. Job spoke of God as the One "who alone stretched out the heavens and trampled the waves of the Sea" (Job 9:8 NRSV). When Jesus calmed the storm, he showed himself to be the answer to the questions in Proverbs 30:4 (NRSV) – "Who has gathered the wind in the hollow of the hand? Who has wrapped up the waters in a garment?" This story graphically demonstrates that God has come down to dwell among human beings.

Why would God come down? Why would he not remain aloof from the messiness of human life, sending his power to fix what people break but never really touching them? Why would the God who can halt the ferocious storm want to reach out to grab Peter's hand when his faith wavered? Why didn't he throw up his hands and rub out this flawed race and start over?

None of us can possibly know the depths of the answer to that question, but the story of Jesus is evidence that he came because he loves us. He loves us so much that he walked dusty roads barefoot just to be with us. He loved us so much that even a leper wasn't too hideous or revolting for him to touch. He loved us so much that he opened himself to betrayal by someone in his closest circle of friends.

Some people have tried to say that Jesus wasn't really God at all. This story refutes that allegation. We can turn to this story for the comfort we need when life is so dark and frightening that we might doubt that God cares. The disciples were at sea at night in a terrible storm, and they were at great risk. We know from experience that a storm at sea can be terrifying, and it only becomes more so in the dark. By 3AM, the time that Jesus was walking on the water out to meet his disciples, a storm-tossed sailor would be yearning for the dawn. Think what it would be like to see an approaching mountain of water, only to watch it subside completely without touching the boat. This is what the disciples observed when Jesus entered their boat with Peter in tow.

God loves the people he created. He has been coming down to tell us so since creation. He came down to talk with Adam and Eve. He came down to talk with Abraham. He came down to talk with Moses and Jonah and the twelve disciples and Mary Magdalene, and he still comes down to each of us. He comes, because he wants a relationship with us. We are important to him.

Reporter Jill Leovy covered the story of D'Angello Mizell, a Crips gang member. In and out of jail from his teen years, he was killed at the age of 36, after being shot three times. His mother, Althea Mizell, mourned his death deeply, even though he had rejected her loving attempts to draw him out of the gang, saying, "The Crips are my mom." The fact that her son rejected her for gang life did not stop her from loving him and mourning his untimely death[1].

God is like that. He doesn't give up on us. We often think to ourselves that we should clean up our lives before meeting him. We think we are too messed up or too dirty or too disorganized. We think we don't have time to get ready for such an encounter. We are wrong. God doesn't care if we are dirty or disheveled or even if we did something bad. He loves us anyway. Jesus who walked on the water and reached out for Peter when he stumbled – that Jesus is ready to walk through fire or flood with each of us, too. God wants a relationship with his children. It is what he lives for.

Day 10

> Out at sea you saw God in action,
> saw his breathtaking ways with the ocean:
> With a word he called up the wind—
> an ocean storm, towering waves!
> You shot high in the sky, then the bottom dropped out;
> your hearts were stuck in your throats.
> You were spun like a top, you reeled like a drunk,
> you didn't know which end was up.
> Then you called out to God in your desperate condition;
> he got you out in the nick of time.
>
> Psalm 107:23-32 MSG

In the book *The Perfect Storm* the author quotes Van Dorn who says, "In violent storms there is so much water in the air, and so much air in the water, that it becomes impossible to tell where the atmosphere stops and the sea begins. That may literally make it impossible to distinguish up from down."[2] We often think that the people who wrote the Psalms were shepherds, but it is obvious that whoever wrote Psalm 107 was intimately acquainted with the sea. Every sailor knows that it is impossible to know enough about the sea. Every sailor knows that the sea demands respect. Every sailor knows that any storm could be fatal. The power with which God has invested the sea is not to be trifled with.

The image of a terrible storm at sea is a perfect image for the terrible storms that arise in our lives. When a child is still-born, when a beloved spouse betrays the marriage, when a child is abused by a parent, when a teen-aged daughter dies of a drug overdose, when a respected pastor succumbs to alcohol – these are situations that can precipitate storms that match the fury of the sea. We feel disoriented and confused. We can't make good decisions – we can't make decisions at all. We toss and turn in the maelstrom of life. We feel that all the anchors and navigation aids are missing. We don't know what to do or how to feel.

We need help. Most likely we cry out, "Oh, God!" but our hearts are not so much praying as accusing. How could this have happened? Why does a good God allow bad things to happen?

The Psalmist testifies that God rescued him in the nick of time. That idea sounds good, but if a child is dead, a spouse has strayed, or the pastor is already in a drunken stupor, we know that the nick of time has already passed. What then?

The answer is not simple. We want simple answers, but we rarely get them. Life is not simple. When a child dies before birth, there are many possible explanations, none of which bring the child to life, many of which can lead a parent down a dark and depressing tunnel of guilt. When a spouse strays, the other spouse feels both angry and guilty. The myriad explanations, justifications and accusations that well up in the face of betrayal only add to the furious confusion of the situation, leading inevitably to a debacle comparable to the image of a ship being pounded into bits by waves against a rocky shore.

Life is complicated. Fixing one thing often breaks something else. It isn't easy to analyze cause and effect when people's choices or failures to choose get mixed up in the results. We shout and curse and plead and cry and collapse. We truly do not know which way is up.

We want God to be there in the nick of time to save us from this trouble. When He seems not to have arrived on time, we turn our fears and accusations against Him, too. How could he let this happen to someone he supposedly loves?

Jesus once felt the same way. Oh, he knew it was coming, that perfect storm that nailed him to a cross. The night before it all came to a head, he prayed to be spared that storm.

"My Father, if there is any way, get me out of this" (Matthew 26:39 MSG). On the cross Jesus cried out, "My God, my God, why have you abandoned me?" (Matthew 27:46 MSG) He knows exactly what it is like to feel alone in the face of disaster.

However, Jesus was not abandoned, and neither are we. The resurrection is the most graphic picture of the hope we have. It also points up an important truth. We are not promised that no bad things will happen, but we are assured that whatever happens, we are not abandoned. On the cross, Jesus joined himself to all our suffering. Nothing we can endure will ever compare with what he endured by taking the sins of the world on himself. The resurrection promises us that nothing we endure can truly defeat us. Martyrs of all ages have testified to their joy in the face of torture and abuse, because they carried that hope in their hearts.

We do not face the storms of the sea or the storms of life alone. The indwelling Holy Spirit is the presence of God with us wherever we go, whatever befalls us. Jesus is always true to his final promise to his followers before his ascension: "I'll be with you as you do this, day after day after day, right up to the end of the age" (Matthew 28:20 MSG).

Day 11

> We stand fearless at the cliff-edge of doom, courageous in sea-storm and earthquake,
>
> Psalm 46:2 MSG

At the 2006 Annapolis Gam of the Seven Seas Cruising Association, one of the guest speakers told of his experience during the tsunami in Banda Aceh in 2004. It was eye-opening. His boat was anchored off one of the islands in the direct path of the tsunami. He and his wife were walking on the beach when the wave arrived. When they realized what was coming, they tried to run away from the wave, but they were caught by the surge. It overpowered them. They were bumped and bruised by debris and completely unable to act against the terrible force of the water. The speaker told of being pushed under the water for such a long time that he began to think he would die. His wife was injured severely as she was tumbled and shoved against objects in the water. They were terrified during the experience and desperate for help afterward. They had a first-hand experience of the scene described by the Psalmist.

The Psalmist, however, says that when we trust in God, we can stand at the edge of doom and be fearless. Is that statement arrogance? Mindless bravado? Stupidity? Wouldn't those who experienced the tsunami feel pretty scornful of anyone who thought he could be fearless in the face of such a thing?

It isn't so much about geological earthquakes as about human quakes. A son deployed to war. A diagnosis of an inoperable tumor. The discovery that executive malfeasance has obliterated a retirement fund. As powerful and devastating as the tsunami was, it doesn't compare with the sight of a state trooper at the door announcing the death of your sixteen-year-old daughter. Living through a tsunami would certainly change anyone, but that experience pales beside the storms that tear families apart and fracture friendships.

In this Psalm, before the writer speaks of the terrible power of the waves, he says, God is a safe place to hide, ready to help when we need him.(Psalm 46:1)

Before the danger appears, we must already know God. He is a safe haven for us, ready when needed, but if we don't know that before the wave hits, how will we know where to go?

This is one of the reasons we spend time daily with God. The time we spend when no danger is evident prepares us to turn to Him when trouble arises. A friend of mine was diagnosed with cancer and began treatment. She told me, and anyone who would listen, that she was as sure of God's presence and power as she fought the cancer as she had ever been in Easter services. After the cancer went into remission and she returned to work, her husband announced that he wanted a divorce. When she told me this, she sounded like a tsunami survivor. Once again, faced with "tremors that shake mountains" she turned to God and hid safely in Him. Because she relied on the Lord before trouble struck, she didn't face the trouble alone. The image the Psalmist gives us reminds us that no matter how faithless we have been, we can run to the Lord, but those who live in relationship with God are already in their safe haven when the storm comes.

As we sail across the seas, we expect to encounter storms. They toss us about and remind us how small we are when compared to the vast ocean of water and air we traverse. We enter alien countries. We hear rumors of piracy and illegitimate arrests. We are always at risk. Yet rooted in our faith that God is present with us at all times, we can face these risks and "stand fearless at the cliff-edge of doom" (Psalm 46:2 MSG).

Day 12

> Happy are those whose help is the God of Jacob,
> whose hope is in the Lord their God,
> who made heaven and earth,
> the sea, and all that is in them;
>
> Psalm 146:5-6 NRSV

Everybody wants to be happy. Advertisers assure us that happiness will be ours if we wear the right clothes, drive the right car, or own the right phone. Motivational speakers tell us that we will be happy if we take charge of our careers or learn how to set our own boundaries. Writers tell us that we will achieve happiness if we have a plan. Fairytales make us yearn for magic lanterns or magic words that will make all our dreams come true.

The common thread is the idea that getting what we want will make us happy. The common truth is that we all know this is a lie.

We hint at the truth when we say, "Be careful what you wish for." The story of King Midas is a poignant reminder that wish fulfillment may have unanticipated and undesirable consequences. However, even when a dream come true is benign, it can still fail to make us happy. Like Dennis the Menace on Christmas morning, we can stand in the midst of abundance and riches and still cry out, "Is that all there is?"

As king of Israel, David had all that his country could offer. He had all the cool possessions and the celebrity status that are reputed to bring happiness. By the popular standards of twenty-first century America, he should have been very happy.

However, David's life was not all bright. Even though he could have had any marriageable woman in the country for a wife, and even though the culture permitted him multiple such wives, he thought he could not be happy without a woman who was someone else's wife. Even though David's children had all the things children could want, their behavior broke his heart over and over. Clearly the possession of riches and power did not produce happiness. David did not write any psalms about how good it felt to be rich and powerful. David did not write psalms about his palace or the land he owned.

David did write psalms of ecstatic happiness. To what did he attribute his happiness? David's happiness was rooted in the God who made sea and land. He rejoiced in the knowledge that the same God who created the universe allowed himself to be known to human beings personally. He recognized that God was high and lifted up, deserving of our worship, yet this God did not stand far off. This God entered into the lives of people. David knew that he could hope in God, not in himself or his accomplishments, and in this hope he found real happiness.

This hope is ours as well. The God of David, the God of Jacob, wants to be our God, too. He wants to know each of us the same way he knew David. He wants to bless us the same way he blessed David. This kind of happiness is quite different from happiness based on popular perceptions. This kind of happiness is fulfilling, and this kind of happiness lasts.

> Praise the Lord!
> Praise the Lord, O my soul!
> I will praise the Lord as long as I live;
> I will sing praises to my God all my life long.
>
> Psalm 146:1-2 NRSV

Day 13

> You will cast all our sins
> into the depths of the sea.
>
> Micah 7:19 NRSV

When we are far at sea, we take advantage of its depths to get rid of unwanted trash. We fill cans and bottles with water and let them fall. When the depthfinder is no longer able to read the real depth and displays only "deep," we know it is safe to let such things go. We will never see them again.

God treats our guilt that way. Who doesn't feel guilty when approaching God? Who among us doesn't look inward and know that we ought to clean up our act before coming anywhere near God? And how about our friends? And our relatives? We have some trashy guilt all mixed up in those relationships, too. Maybe we even feel guilty about who we are or who we never became. Some of us can't even say why we feel guilty. We just know something isn't right somewhere.

Our guilt motivates strange behaviors. We think we want reconciliation with God and our friends, but our guilty feelings make us turn away. We run from the ones we yearn for. We avoid God, family, friends. We think we need to get straightened out first, but we can't straighten ourselves out at all. Guilt becomes a prison we cannot escape.

Into this prison a light shines. God's grace reaches down to us. His forgiveness wipes away the burden and breaks down the walls. All because Jesus died for us.

It's a wonder God didn't lose his temper and do away with the whole lot of us. Instead, with immense mercy and incredible love, he embraced us. He took our sin-dead lives and made us alive in Christ. He did all this on his own, with no help from us!

Nothing compares to the experience of being forgiven. The guilt and anger and pain simply peel off and fall away. They are gone. The world is full of light. The very air nourishes hope. Suddenly anything is possible.

Where is the god who can compare with you— wiping a slate clean of guilt, turning a blind eye, a deaf ear, to the past sins of your purged and precious people? You don't nurse your anger and don't stay angry long, for mercy is your specialty. That's what you love most. And compassion is on its way to us. You'll stamp out our wrongdoing. You'll sink our sins to the bottom of the ocean.

You'll stay true to your word to Father Jacob and continue the compassion you showed Grandfather Abraham— Everything you promised our ancestors from a long time ago.

Micah 7:18-20

Day 14

> Surely, this commandment that I am commanding you today is not too hard for you, nor is it too far away. It is not in heaven, that you should say, "Who will go up to heaven for us, and get it for us so that we may hear it and observe it?" Neither is it beyond the sea, that you should say, "Who will cross to the other side of the sea for us, and get it for us so that we may hear it and observe it?" No, the word is very near to you; it is in your mouth and in your heart for you to observe.
>
> Deuteronomy 30:11-14 NRSV

It is common to hear someone say that he is seeking truth, or trying to find God, or hopes to return to his roots. Someone who makes a pilgrimage is usually trying to find a place where God or Truth or Wisdom will be closer, more accessible. When Moses made his farewell to the Israelites, many no doubt worried that with Moses gone God might be gone, too. As Moses spoke, he reassured them that God was not far away. Just as Jesus later said to people, "The kingdom of God is among you" (Luke 17:21 NRSV), Moses said, "The word is right here and now" (Deuteronomy 30:14 MSG).

Many people believe that we must do something extraordinary in order to be close to God. People are wrong about that. God is always close to us. He came down to walk with Adam and Eve. He came down to talk with Moses in the burning bush. He lived among the Israelites in the wilderness. He was right there, not far away. The Bible says that God is the one who does the extraordinary things for a relationship with people. In Jesus, God came down and lived among us in the flesh. We don't need to go running or sailing or trekking in order to find God. He is right here.

People who have done wrong know this truth. They feel pursued by judgment on their actions. We have all been there. In fact, talk show hosts profit greatly from people willing to talk about that feeling. That guilt is the voice of God's presence among us. It reminds us that we need him. However, making us feel guilty is not God's greatest desire. What he really wants is a relationship of faith and love.

It should be reassuring to know that. God is as near as our own bodies. We don't need to seek Him, because he sought us first. We are never really alone. The apostle Paul wrote to the Romans, and reminded them of this truth when he quoted Moses, "The word is near you, on your lips and in your heart" ([Romans 10:8 NRSV).

It is a human trait to delight in mysteries and puzzles. Books such as *The DaVinci Code* and *The Secret* intrigue readers who would prefer to believe that God hides his truth in puzzles and tests. Many people believe that God will only tell his truth to selected special people who will then tell some of that truth to the rest of us. Every religion has priests with secrets, except Christianity. The Bible tells us over and over that God is not like that. He won't try to test our intelligence before he tells us his truth. He lays it out plainly. He writes it on our hearts. He makes each of us his priest. He lives within each of us.

In our relationships with each other, we can find evidence that if our natural inclinations prevailed in our relationship with God, it would be different. When we feel hurt or shut out by others, we want some payback. Even if we don't get it, we feel entitled to it, and when we "forgive" someone, we want credit for not demanding anything. It is a good thing that God does not treat us the same way. In fact, when we see Jesus on the cross, we can see that God yearned so much to be reconciled with us that he took all the payback for the whole human race on himself. He didn't ask us to make it up to him because we are so fickle and faithless and selfish; he made it up himself. He didn't ask us to cry and pray and weep endlessly because we don't deserve his love; he did all that for us, and he did it very publicly. It wasn't done in a corner. He doesn't ask us to do extraordinary things in order to be his friend; he does extraordinary things in order to be a friend to us.

God wants a relationship with people. When he created people, he breathed into each one his own breath. We all rejoice at the first cry of a baby, because the baby must breathe. In that moment we can almost see God leaning down lovingly over his creation, administering mouth-to-mouth resuscitation, breathing into this new baby his own breath, his own Spirit. God really is near us all our lives -- "as near as the tongue in your mouth, as near as the heart in your chest" (Deuteronomy 30:14 MSG).

Day 15

> God-of-the-Angel-Armies,
> who is like you, powerful and faithful from every angle?
> You put the arrogant ocean in its place
> and calm its waves when they turn unruly.
> …You own the cosmos—you made everything in it,
> everything from atom to archangel.
>
> Psalm 89:8-11 MSG

The Bible records that we humans are invited to approach God and bring to him all our concerns. It would be easy to think that this is an invitation to whine. It is not. This psalm reminds us who God is. When we contemplate who he truly is, then we know that our right to approach him is not trivial. When Matthew Henry read this psalm, he suggested that we think carefully about our attitude in prayer. He said we should watch ourselves, in order that the "familiarity we are admitted to may not breed the least contempt."[3] We are invited into God's presence, but we are enjoined by his majesty to show respect.

Why should we respect God? This psalm points out that the most ungovernable object on earth, the very ocean, is subject to God. Sailors learn early that they must respect the ocean, because it does what it wants. The ocean, however, must respect God, because he can shut it down if it turns unruly. This God can put the brakes or the accelerator on a tsunami.

For that matter, the psalmist points out a bigger truth, that nothing in the universe is outside God's ownership and control. God makes and disposes of all the amazing and wonderful objects in the Hubble telescope photographs. "You own the cosmos—you made everything in it, everything from atom to archangel" (Psalm 89:11MSG).

Yet this is the God who comes down to seek our company. It isn't easy to reconcile these two images – the transcendent and powerful creator of everything and the loving shepherd who leaves ninety-nine in the fold while he goes after one that is lost. It is humbling to consider what this means.

Viewed from the deck of a boat, both sea and land look quite different than they appear from the middle of a town or from a car traveling a freeway. That perspective is a great leveler. It is easier to see how land and sea are part of one great cosmic truth. The psalmist reminds me that my cosmic view is like a single windowpane in God's view, for he sees all and knows all. He knows creation the way I know the soup whose flavor I built layer by layer until it was very good. God sees his creation as good, but it is not free to defy him. All creation is still under his control.

When I consider that the God who made mountains and waves and stars actually cares enough to listen to my prayer, I know that I owe him both respect and obedience. Prayer to this God is not like sitting on Santa's lap at the mall. I can come to God as his child, but like a child, I owe my Heavenly Father respect.

Day 16

> Who shut in the sea with doors ...
> and said, 'Thus far shall you come, and no farther,
> and here shall your proud waves be stopped'?
>
> Job 38:8,11NRSV

When Job lost everything after God set Satan free to torment him, three friends came to sit with him in his misery. Ostensibly, they came to comfort him, but in fact, their mission appeared to be an investigation. They pressed Job to confess his bad behavior that had motivated God to punish him. They thought they knew what was in God's mind. Job's response was an impassioned protest of innocence, and eventually he wore himself out, declaring he wished he had never been born. He cried out for God to face him and answer his questions. When God did speak, he first reprimanded the false friends and praised Job's truthful remarks. Then God turned to Job. Job had spoken truth about God, as far as he went, but he had spoken without respect, treating God like an equal who could be called to account for what he had done. In the verses above, God reminds Job that the Creator does not need to justify himself to the creature.

Although the Bible includes a creation story, every reader knows that no human was there to observe. God acted without input from anyone to create the universe, and our most ambitious explorations only make it more obvious that we know very little about its workings. After listening to Job and his supposed friends, God speaks out in these verses to remind Job of the limits of his knowledge.

As a child, much of my social life was spent with family and friends of my parents. They had all known me since I was born. Sometimes, I thought they knew entirely too much about me. This is the way God can look at the ocean. When God looks at it, his knowledge is not limited. He not only knows what it is today. He also knows what it was when time began.

Recognizing the vast difference between the way God sees time and space and the way we see it should put us in awe of God. Humans imagine and build some really massive projects, but they hardly make a flyspeck on the earth when viewed from God's perspective. The teachings about God's love and grace do not change who God is. Rather, recognition of who God is increases our gratitude and humility for those great gifts.

This is real wisdom – to recognize who God really is. He isn't a buddy who makes things nice for us. He doesn't forgive us just so we can all get along. He is the Creator. He made the rules. The laws scientists keep discovering are His laws. We may think we can flout God's laws about our behavior without consequence, but we should recognize that the God who spoke the law of gravity into existence also said, "I am the Lord your God…you shall have no other gods before me" (Exodus 20:2-3 NRSV). He is the God who brought forth the oceans, and all the myriad objects of the cosmos. God loves us, but he is not to be trifled with.

Day 17

> God claims Earth and everything in it,
> God claims World and all who live on it.
> He built it on Ocean foundations,
> laid it out on River girders.
>
> Psalm 24:1 MSG

Viewing things in the light of our own experience, we might ask ourselves why God would build anything on water. It is not a steady underpinning. It moves constantly. Even a child can push through it. If a person whispers close to the surface of water, the movement of the air will ripple the water.

Yet water has power that nothing can resist. The people faced with the Banda Aceh tsunami of 2004 can attest to that truth. On that day, water piled up in mountains and crushed structures the way we might wad a piece of waste paper.

Hydraulic engineers know that water has a powerful property: it forcibly resists compression. They use this property to lift massive objects against the inexorable force of gravity. In water, God created something that can be stirred by a feather, but can't be compressed by a bulldozer. God's universe is mysterious and wonderful, and we have not yet probed all its secrets.

Since God is the perfect and transcendent king over all, the Psalm writer asks, "Who can climb Mount God?" (Psalm 24:3 MSG) He is asking who dares to enter into God's presence, and the answer is, people of integrity. "Men who won't cheat, women who won't seduce" (Psalm 24:4 MSG). The Bible repeatedly uses images of marriage and adultery to describe the behavior of people in their relationships with God. When the author of Revelation tries to describe what will happen when the new heaven and earth come to pass, he calls the church the bride of Christ. When the prophets needed to make it clear to Israel how far she had fallen from the relationship God intended at Sinai, they called the behavior of the Israelites "whoredom." If we want to approach God, we must live with integrity. Integrity is a way of living that does not cave under pressure, just as water is not compressed by being stepped on. Integrity is a perfect life. Nobody can live such a life. We are all doomed. Nobody can climb Mount God.

Can we ever wash our hands and our hearts sufficiently to be worthy to approach God? The Psalmist points out that we cannot do it by ourselves. He says, "God is at their side; with God's help they make it" (Psalm 24:5 MSG) The Psalmist points us to Jesus, the author and finisher of our salvation. Our hands and hearts only become clean and pure when we are washed in the blood of our Savior. We can come to God, because we are cleansed by Him.

Each time we observe The Lord's Supper, we are reminded that Jesus is our only hope. The forgiveness that enables us to approach God is purchased by the broken body and shed blood of Christ. In the sacrament of the Lord's Supper, we are nourished by Christ's body and blood, we are kept in His grace, and we are made ready to approach God.

Day 18

> Do you realize where you are? You're in a cosmos star-flung with constellations by God, A world God wakes up each morning and puts to bed each night. God dips water from the ocean and gives the land a drink. God, God-revealed, does all this. And he can destroy it as easily as make it. He can turn this vast wonder into total waste.
>
> Amos 5:8-9 MSG

Who do you think you are? You will hear these words when someone believes you have transgressed by failing to show proper respect. When a child talks back to his mother, when a servant refuses to obey her master, when a pipsqueak nation presumes to affront a global power, these are the words that might be spoken or shouted.

Amos is the voice of God speaking, or shouting as necessary, to people who have forgotten both who God is and who they are. The people of Israel, who were led lovingly through the wilderness to the Promised Land, who were taught by Moses to leave something behind for the poor during harvest, who were told that God demands truth from their lips – these people now trample the poor and abhor the truth. They use God's laws to benefit themselves, not to serve God. Amos confronts them with straight talk.

People hate this kind of talk. Raw truth is never popular. But here it is, bluntly spoken:

> Because you run roughshod over the poor and take the bread right out of their mouths, You're never going to move into the luxury homes you have built. You're never going to drink wine from the expensive vineyards you've planted. I know precisely the extent of your violations, the enormity of your sins. Appalling!   Amos 5:10-11a MSG

People who try to fool God are a lot like a child who thinks he can fool his mother. They do not realize that they will be found out. In these verses, God reminds Israel who he is and who they are. He points out that the whole universe is His creation. It is completely at His disposal. A mother might say to a wild child, "I brought you into this world, and I can take you out." Amos reminds Israel that God can destroy their world as easily as he made it. He can turn his beautiful, thriving creation, and the Promised Land within it, into a total waste.

The people to whom Amos spoke used the phrase "God is with us" very much as my high school used the mantra "Bulldogs are the best!" They thought of this phrase as a lucky charm, an incantation that manipulated God. God hated their religiosity, which only thinly disguised their scorn for him and the greed that drove their behavior.

> Listen to this, you who walk all over the weak, you who treat poor people as less than nothing, Who say, "When's my next paycheck coming so I can go out and live it up? How long till the weekend when I can go out and have a good time?" ... You exploit the poor, using them—and then, when they're used up, you discard them...."On Judgment Day, watch out!" These are the words of God, my Master.
>
> Amos 8:4-7, 9a MSG

As God's spokesman, Amos shouted his message, calling the children of Israel back, pleading with them to return to the God who loved them. God yearned for his children to come home, like any mother does. Amos spoke harsh words and sounded dire warnings, because God wanted to be reconciled with his alienated people. When Jonah shouted at Nineveh, the people repented, and God cancelled their harsh punishment. God wanted the same result when he sent Amos to speak to Israel.

A friend who taught English composition to college freshmen was much in demand for her outstanding teaching skills and her track record of inspiring students to achieve excellence. A small university recruited her to replace a professor who had not upheld the high standards my friend demanded of her students.

Her new students almost universally hated her. Students who previously could whip out a paper while riding back to campus after a long weekend found that their lack of effort was recognized and reprimanded by a fierce red pen. When mid-term grades were posted, many students were shocked at how far they had fallen below her expectations. One of them said to her, "I bet they brought you in just to make it hard for us."

The Israelites thought of Amos the same way. He was very annoying. He presumed to call into question a way of life that was quite comfortable for some of the people. They thought he was doing it just to be irritating.

Like the teacher who wanted her students to excel in composition, Amos wanted the Israelites to excel in obedience to God. He didn't rebuke wealth because it was wealth, but rather because it was obtained at the price of flouting everything God expected of His people. When Moses delivered his farewell address in the wilderness, he virtually promised the Israelites an affluent society, so it is clear that affluence in itself was not the evil Amos deplored. Rather, Amos deplored, in the name of God, arrogant disregard for the poor, the sick and the weak. He deplored a society that revered the lie and scorned the truth. He abhorred the deliberate thievery practiced by merchants, government, and even priests to enrich themselves by "skimping the measure, boosting the price, and cheating with dishonest scales" (Amos 8:5b NRSV).

The message of God's forgiveness through Christ is very comforting. No experience compares to the feeling when our guilt is washed away in the blood of Christ. We rightly rejoice in the discovery that we can fail and try again and fail and try again like children learning to walk. However, we must remember the price of our forgiveness -- the cross. Our forgiveness is not a license to continue in behaviors that require forgiveness. Jesus purchased our forgiveness in order that we might be free to live differently. Jesus, like Amos, said that our behavior is significant. Our commitment to justice for the poor and the weak is as important for us today as it was for the ancient Israelites to whom Amos spoke. Amos, God's prophet to Israel, said, "Do you know what I want? I want justice—oceans of it. I want fairness—rivers of it"(Amos 5:24 MSG).

Jesus, the Son of God, said,

Then those "goats" are going to say, 'Master, what are you talking about? When did we ever see you hungry or thirsty or homeless or shivering or sick or in prison and didn't help?' He will answer them, 'I'm telling the solemn truth: Whenever you failed to do one of these things to someone who was being overlooked or ignored, that was me—you failed to do it to me.' Then those "goats" will be herded to their eternal doom, but the "sheep" to their eternal reward.

Matthew 25:44-56 MSG

Day 19

> Why don't you honor me? Why aren't you in awe before me? Yes, me, who made the shorelines to contain the ocean waters. I drew a line in the sand that cannot be crossed. Waves roll in but cannot get through; breakers crash but that's the end of them.
>
> Jeremiah 5:22 MSG

When it is time to elect a new president for the United States, a lot of people line up to be candidates. Some who are not serious candidates present themselves publicly to promote an agenda they know is not popular simply because a presidential candidate can get a hearing. Most candidates, however, look for a way to make themselves attractive to voters. The team that supports each candidate spends a great deal of time and effort trying to find ways for the candidate to say what everyone wants to hear. Voters, on the other hand, yearn for someone who will speak and act with truth.

God loves truth. God also loves lives that are consistent with truth, lives of integrity. When he sees leaders spreading lies that deceive and rob the people they should serve, he is outraged. We may have trouble decoding their message, but God is not fooled.

> Indeed, there are wicked scoundrels among my people. They lie in wait like bird catchers hiding in ambush. They set deadly traps to catch people. Like a cage filled with the birds that have been caught, their houses are filled with the gains of their fraud and deceit. That is how they have gotten so rich and powerful. Jeremiah 5:26-27 NET

Most voters have seen elected officials betray everything in their campaign platform after the election is over. We have all observed the "wicked scoundrels" Jeremiah is talking about. We have been ambushed by lies and deceit. We have been caught and imprisoned by government actions that defraud us of the very benefits government is supposed to give us – freedom, opportunity, and the right to fail without punishment. We have all seen politicians use their elected office to enrich themselves while they ignored the real needs of the people they were elected to serve.

We have also seen the hangers-on. Those are the people who join the politicians in order to make themselves rich, powerful, and important. These camp followers work within all the shady deals, believing that they are clever enough to swindle the swindlers. In this way, citizens are doubly defrauded, first by their leaders and then by their neighbors.

This kind of behavior angers God. His anger should both encourage us and warn us. He is not fooled by human deceit and fraud. This God, who is able to set limits on the sea, sets limits on people, too. The God who can say to a vast ocean, "This far and no farther," can reach down and punish greed, lies and deceit. The God who can turn mountainous breakers into nothing at the limit of the shore can absolutely deal with treacherous leadership. When we read this passage, we should be both reassured and warned that God will act against those who trifle with His plan for the world

This passage again reminds us that the image being sold to us daily by the ever-present media is not the image God wants for our lives. We are led to believe that it is actually important to dress in the finest clothes, or to be the most entertaining, or to have the most money. God says that all these things are like nothing, worse than nothing. What matters to him is justice in public life. What is each of us doing to meet the needs of the poor, the orphans, the oppressed? In the kingdom of God, the last will be first, the greatest will be servant of all, and the least will be Jesus in our presence.

God wants us to respect his vision of what is good for us. He spoke to the Israelites through the prophets, then he spoke through conquerors, then he spoke through Jesus. Do we dare ignore him?

> Thunder crashes and rumbles in the skies.
> Listen! It's God raising his voice!
> By his power he stills sea storms,
> by his wisdom he tames sea monsters.
> With one breath he clears the sky,
> with one finger he crushes the sea serpent.
> And this is only the beginning,
> a mere whisper of his rule.
> Whatever would we do if he really raised his voice!
>
> Job 26:11-14 MSG

Day 20

> God is King, robed and ruling, God is robed and surging with strength. And yes, the world is firm, immovable, your throne ever firm—you're Eternal! Sea storms are up, God, sea storms wild and roaring, sea storms with thunderous breakers. Stronger than wild sea storms, mightier than sea-storm breakers, mighty God rules from High Heaven. What you say goes—it always has. "Beauty" and "Holy" mark your palace rule, God, to the very end of time.
>
> Psalm 93:1-5 MSG

If God is mightier than the waves of the sea, then He is mighty, indeed. We know what the waves of the sea can do to a small boat. Even an aircraft carrier seems small when tossed by the power of the waves. However, if God is mightier than the waves, then he is also mightier than life's tragedies. Sometimes those waves rock us more forcefully than the wildest storm at sea. A young life snuffed out by mindless violence. A baby who dies before he is born. A wife humiliated and oppressed by a husband's vengeful ego. A parent who slips away into the dark night of dementia. These waves rock us like no mere ocean can possibly do. They shatter our ability to cope. They drain our faith and crush hope.

These are the mighty waves that really threaten to destroy us. When this sort of wave engulfs us, we need to know that God is "robed in majesty" and "girded with strength." We need to know that he is "from everlasting." Only something infinite and omnipotent can possibly defeat the destruction wrought in our spirits when the real waves roll over us. In that hour we truly need to know that God is mightier than all these destructive waves that assault us.

When Jesus was about to be crucified, he told his disciples, "Peace I leave with you; my peace I give to you. I do not give to you as the world gives. Do not let your hearts be troubled, and do not let them be afraid" (John 14:27 NIV84). He gave this gift in the context of the gift of the indwelling Holy Spirit. He promised his disciples that the Holy Spirit within would be the power within them. At Pentecost, they learned what Jesus meant. The power of the almighty God, more powerful than ocean waves, had been given to them. They did not go forth to calm the oceans of the world; they went forth to bring peace to people rocked by the daily tragedies of human life.

This is the real consolation of Psalm 93. When we know the truth of God's character, then we can join with the psalmist in praise. Praise is our natural response to knowledge of God. It is the most acceptable sacrifice we can bring. Blessed and indwelt by the power of Almighty God, we can sing with the psalmist: "Holiness befits your house, O Lord, forevermore" (Psalm 93:5 NRSV).

Day 21

> What's wrong with you, Sea, that you ran away? and you, River Jordan, that you turned and ran off?
> And mountains, why did you skip like rams? and you, hills, frolic like spring lambs?
> Tremble, Earth! You're in the Lord's presence! in the presence of Jacob's God.
> He turned the rock into a pool of cool water, turned flint into fresh spring water.
>
> Psalm 114:5-8 MSG

This playful poem sounds almost trivial on first reading. One wonders what it is doing in the hymnbook of the ages. Casual examination makes the reader ask, how does it end? A closer, more attentive look finds a beautiful song, complete in every way, a powerful statement of faith.

The Bible makes it clear that when we try to fit God into a human image of the world, He bursts out like a child trying to wear last year's shirt. God is not like us. He is so unlike us that everything he does seems upside down. He honors the poor and the weak while punishing the rich and powerful. He stands fluid waters on end and makes solid mountains sway.

This Psalm is a celebration of the beautiful truth that God is not like us. If he were, we would have no hope, nothing to celebrate. God can turn rock into water for the people to drink. God turns the sea into a wall that marks a path where people walk on dry land. This is a God in whom we can rejoice. What can He not do?

Read the Psalm. Shut out everything else. Listen to it in your head and your heart. Let go of your surroundings and the limitations of your humanity. Let your heart dance before the Lord like the mountains. Let your spirit sing to him and rejoice in who He is. He is the Lord. Show respect and delight at the same time.

Day 22

> And Ezra said:? "You are the Lord, you alone; you have made heaven, the heaven of heavens, with all their host, the earth and all that is on it, the seas and all that is in them. To all of them you give life, and the host of heaven worships you.
>
> Nehemiah 9:6 NRSV

This text is the prayer of a people who had looked at themselves in God's mirror, and they did not like what they saw. Ezra spoke words of worship and praise to the God who had created everything. When the people realized who God was, they immediately realized that they did not deserve to be his chosen people.

The people were confronted with a reality they had forgotten: God is omnipotent and worthy of worship and praise. He is not a genie who grants three wishes. We owe him our reverence. We must be honest with him about who we are. It is God's nature to expect perfect obedience, but it is also part of his nature to give us grace and forgiveness. They knew that they needed to confess their sins, but even before they did that, they needed to praise him. Their words of praise were their acknowledgement that they needed to confess their sins.

Over and over in the Bible, when people have wandered away from God and then turn around to contemplate what they have done, they are struck first by the difference between God and themselves. They praise him first, and then confess their sins.

In this text, the Ezra praised God for his gift of life. The sea displays God's gift of life in a richness and diverse beauty that puts land-based life forms in the shade. God's gift of life is amazing and powerful. Life is able to thrive and flourish in conditions we can't imagine. Every time we think we know the limits of life, we discover that life can thrive where it is too dark, too cold, too hot, too dry, too wet, too oxygen-poor, too dense due to water pressure, and so forth. God is able to produce and support life far beyond our ability to understand how that works. The richest gift he gives to all of us is eternal life with him, the source of all life.

What is eternal life? What does it mean? When we can't even comprehend earthly life, what makes us think we can comprehend eternal life? Life without end. I am personally sure that it isn't a bland existence – walking golden streets, playing golden harps, flying from cloud to cloud. The life we have here is a constant challenge. We grow by overcoming our challenges, and we certainly know that we do it by the grace and power of God, yet it only happens if we get ready and do it. There is a mystery between the decision of faith and the act of God. I can't believe for a minute that this mystery is less rich in the next iteration of life.

Day 23

> You have been just in all that has come upon us, for you have dealt faithfully and we have acted wickedly.
>
> Nehemiah 9:33 NRSV

The book of Nehemiah is a caution. On the one hand, it is comforting to see that a large number of people were willing to leave Babylon and return to the land of Israel, their homeland. Few of the people who returned had ever lived in that country. They only knew what their parents and grandparents had told them about it. They knew the stories of how God had judged the people and had sent them into exile for their disobedience. This return was supposedly an act of faith and commitment to right the wrongs that had resulted in God's punishment.

The prayer recorded in Nehemiah 9 is fervent. It confesses sin and commits to amendment of life. After the prayer, there is a written covenant with God in which the people promise to live by God's law and reject the sins of their ancestors. It sounds like a very happy occasion.

Yet, as soon as Nehemiah leaves to report to King Artaxerxes that his mission has been accomplished, the covenant ends. Tobiah, who must have been a smarmy politician, persuades the Levites to give him a room in the newly-restored temple. He takes the space that was dedicated to storing the temple vessels and the gifts of the people. Those items must have been scattered disrespectfully hither and thither. The great commitment to worship and service was dead already.

Further, all the promises to honor and preserve the immediately. Not only do Gentile merchants freely buy and sell on the Sabbath, but the Israelites join in the trading frenzy. They don't want to be left out of the profits!

When Nehemiah returns from Babylon, he discovers what has happened and takes immediate action to restore faithful observance of God's law. By the end of the book, the people are once again worshiping and serving the God who created the seas and walks on the waves. Yet, an attentive reader will quietly wonder how long it will take for another Tobiah to show up.

They aren't so different from us. Don't we enjoy the celebration of Christmas more than the dark days of Lent? Don't we like giving and getting gifts more than denying self and getting real about sin? We love to sing "Eternal Father Strong to Save" more than "Hymn of Confession." We can proudly sing "Send Me, O Lord, Send Me," but at the end of the service we really only want to be sent to the dinner table. The fact that the God who created heaven and earth, sky and sea, wants faithful, obedient service to Him is much less important to us than setting priorities that build our careers and earn money. Even if we are cruising the wide oceans, we tend to be immersed in the personal gratification of the adventure; we aren't actually looking around to see if we can help someone in need. We may praise God for the wind and wave, but we don't want to give up our plan for fun in order to serve him. We really aren't much different from the ancient Israelites.

Day 24

> Praise the Lord from the heavens;
> Praise him in the heights!
> Praise him, all his angels;
> Praise him, all his host!
>
> Psalm 148:1-2 NRSV

When we have a relationship with God, when we get to know him in all his glory, then we want to praise him. We recognize how inadequate we are to praise him, because he transcends anything we can imagine. We call on all of creation to join us in praising him. Anything less seems too little.

God, however, does not need our praise. He is completely sufficient to himself. He needs nothing. He did not need the sacrifices of the Israelites, and he does not need for us to praise what he does. We do not meet his need when we praise him. We meet our own need, because his presence calls forth praise. We might try to be silent, but we cannot.

In Psalm 39, the writer stands before God and feels so thoroughly humbled that he says, "I will put a muzzle on my mouth" (Psalm 39:1 NIV84). He stands silent as long as he can, but then "as I meditated, the fire burned; then I spoke with my tongue" (Psalm 39:3 NIV84)

The psalmist's reverent silence before the Lord as one unworthy to speak ends when prayer explodes from his soul. He says, "My hope is in you. Save me from all my transgressions" (Psalm 39:7-8 NIV84). His silence has become praise.

Therefore, we invite everything God has created to join us in praising him. From the depths of the ocean to the height of the heavens.

> Praise the Lord from the earth,
> you sea monsters and all deeps,
> fire and hail, snow and frost,
> stormy wind fulfilling his command!
>
> Psalm 148:7-8 NRSV

As we traverse the oceans, we encounter all sorts of living creatures. Life is powerful. God has put life everywhere on earth. Dolphins that play in the bow wave. Flying fish who leap across the deck. Petrels that dance on the crests of waves. Gulls that screech and circle the boat. Jellyfish. Whales. Corals. Sponges. Parrotfish who make the sand on a thousand seashores. Life, amazing life, mysterious life, beautiful, fantastic, almost magical life. Can we ever unravel the mystery? Is it even possible to find words adequate to praise the God who could create this miracle?

> Let them praise the name of the Lord,
> for his name alone is exalted;
> his glory is above earth and heaven.
>
> Psalm 148:13 NRSV

Day 25

> To the one who divided the Red Sea in two, for his loyal love endures
>
> Psalm 136:13 NET

Psalm 136 is a paean of praise and thanksgiving to God. The "loyal love" for which thanks is given is expressed in Hebrew by the word *hesed*. The more common translations of this word into English are *lovingkindness, steadfast love, grace* and *mercy*. *Loyalty* is a less common translation. The many variants point up the difficulty in making this single Hebrew word comprehensible in a single English word or phrase.

More than one book has been devoted to studying the Hebrew word *hesed*. It is a key word for Old Testament study, but in few texts is its meaning so integral to the whole as in this Psalm. Here, the meaning of *hesed* is the seasoning that gives the Psalm its real flavor. The phrase "for [*hesed*] endures" recurs in every line of the Psalm. Obviously it is a congregational response in a worship litany, but the phrase was not chosen because it was easy for the congregation to remember. This phrase glues every thought in the Psalm to a single reason for giving thanks. No matter what specific incident might provoke thanksgiving, the Psalmist points to a single explanation for that incident: *hesed*.

Translators struggle with the richness and nuance of this word. The Rabbinic studies which point up the mutuality of the word shine real light on the Psalm. *Hesed*, they say, is not a monolithic attitude. At its core, it is part of the covenant relationship with Israel. *Hesed* describes actions that are undertaken within a mutual relationship. Yet, when we look at God's acts and Israel's acts, we see clearly that God's grace to Israel, like his grace to us, is very often unilateral. If he waited for us to participate fully in the "mutual" behavior and attitudes, he might wait a very long time.

This word calls us back to the establishment of God's covenant with Abram. In Genesis 15, we find that story:

> Then [God] said to [Abram], "I am the Lord who brought you from Ur of the Chaldeans, to give you this land to possess." But he said, "O Lord God, how am I to know that I shall possess it?" He said to him, "Bring me a heifer three years old, a female goat three years old, a ram three years old, a turtledove, and a young pigeon." He brought him all these and cut them in two, laying each half over against the other; but he did not cut the birds in two. And when birds of prey came down on the carcasses, Abram drove them away. ... When the sun had gone down and it was dark, a smoking fire pot and a flaming torch passed between these pieces. On that day the Lord made a covenant with Abram.
>
> Genesis 15:7-11, 17-18 NRSV

According to ancient practice, two people who established a "covenant" or "contract" relationship used the ritual of passing between the pieces of the severed animal parts to seal the contract. In the action of this ritual each party was saying, "If I break the terms of this covenant, may it be with me as with these bloodied beasts."

When God "contracted" with Abram to be his God, Abram stood by and watched. Only God passed through the animal parts. Only God agreed to accept the punishment for breaking the contract. When the psalmist in Psalm 136 says, "Give thanks to the Lord, for he is good, for his loyal love endures" (Psalm 136:1 NET), he is giving thanks for the fact that God always lives up to his part of that one-sided contract. Israel prided itself on being God's covenant people, but Israel never really agreed to take the consequences of failure. The Bible records that there were times when God allowed terrible things to happen to Israel, but if we look at those stories closely, we see at the root of the horror God's cry to his people, "Return, return." None of the "punishment" Israel received was ever meant to abrogate the covenant God had made. Jesus on the cross tells us that God took the consequences of the broken covenant completely upon himself.

Psalm 136 is certainly a hymn of praise, but it also a reassurance. We can count on God. He invites us into relationship with him, even though he knows before he asks that we can't live up to that invitation. He knows we are dust. He knows we are frail. Therefore, he invites us into a loving relationship and absorbs all the punishment. He came down in the flesh to show us the depth of his commitment to this relationship. We can count on God, no matter how many times we fail. His loyal love endures every failure on our part and acts with strength in our lives.

> Give thanks to the Lord, for he is good, for his loyal love endures.
> Give thanks to the God of gods, for his loyal love endures.
> Give thanks to the Lord of lords, for his loyal love endures,
> To the one who performs magnificent, amazing deeds all by himself, for his loyal love endures.
> Psalm 136:1-4 NET

Day 26

Wherever the river flows, life will flourish

Ezekiel 47:9 MSG

This statement is found in the depths of a beautiful passage that describes a vision God gave to Ezekiel. It is filled with imagery of a great river that flows from God's heavenly temple into all the earth, bringing life wherever it goes. The passage says that "Fishermen will stand shoulder to shoulder along the shore from En-gedi all the way north to En-eglaim, casting their nets. The sea will teem with fish of all kinds" (Ezekiel 47:10 MSG). We are reminded that Jesus told his disciples that they would become "fishers of men." This image calls to mind the story after Christ's resurrection when he told them to "Throw your net on the right side of the boat" (John 21:6 NIV84), and they pulled in a catch so large that the nets threatened to break.

The river in Ezekiel brings life. The image of this life-giving water reminds us of baptism in which we are buried to sin and raised to new life in Christ. That water changes everything, just like the water of Ezekiel's river. When I remember my baptism, I remember this life-giving truth. We are reborn with real life into the family of Jesus, the firstborn of God and firstborn of the family of God, marked by baptism.

When Jesus was ready to start his ministry, he went to John to be baptized. John felt unworthy of this task, as well he might. He knew who Jesus was, and he knew that for him to baptize Jesus had the appearance of making him more important than Jesus. Later John said of himself and Jesus, "He [meaning Jesus] must increase, but I must decrease" (John 3:30 NRSV). Why, then, did Jesus say that it was important for him to be baptized. In so doing, he emphasized a couple of important truths. First, the person who conducts baptism is an ordinary human being with no special powers. As the earthly agent of baptism, he is simply obedient to the command of God. Second, it is not the baptizer, but God himself, who marks the one baptized as belonging to God Himself forever.

Baptism is important, because it is God's act. God himself marks every human being that belongs to him in this way. It shows other people that we belong to God. It unites us with all who were baptized before us. Most important, it wipes away the death sentence of sin and raises us up into eternal life with Christ. As the firstborn of the family of God, Jesus submitted to baptism, becoming completely one with the entire human race, despite his sinlessness. Had he not become one in baptism with us, his death on the cross would have been meaningless. Instead of the sacrifice of the sinless one for all the sinners, it would have been either the pointless, painless symbolic death of a god or it would have been the cruel torture of one who was no different from the criminals on either side of him. In baptism, Jesus joined himself to the redeemed of all ages.

When Jesus entered the waters of Jordan to be baptized by John, he was already marked for the cross. It was his destiny. When I entered the waters of baptism, I, too, was marked for the cross. I was united with Christ's death that redeemed me from sin and joined to his resurrected life. Baptism is all about life. Real life. Life that rejoices. Life that is full of energy, excitement and hope. Life that floods forth like a river.

Day 27

> Shout Bravo! to his famous Name, lift high an offering and enter his presence! Stand resplendent in his robes of holiness!
> God is serious business, take him seriously; he's put the earth in place and it's not moving.
> So let Heaven rejoice, let Earth be jubilant, and pass the word among the nations, "God reigns!"
> Let Ocean, all teeming with life, bellow, let Field and all its creatures shake the rafters;
> Then the trees in the forest will add their applause to all who are pleased and present before God —he's on his way to set things right!
> Give thanks to God—he is good and his love never quits.
>
> I Chronicles 16:29-34 MSG

In 1633 Galileo stood trial because, in an alleged contradiction to biblical teaching, he had written that the earth moved around the sun. The text quoted above from I Chronicles, among others, was used to convict him of heresy that he was required to recant. It is a prime example of an attempt to use the Bible as a book about science rather than as a book about God. Galileo later wrote that the Bible was written to tell people how to go to heaven, not how the heavens go, but the idea of a universe that did not revolve around an immobile earth continued to be rejected as unscriptural for many years afterward

As ! Chronicles 16 opens, David has brought the Ark into Jerusalem. The Ark had been in virtual exile at Kiriath-Jearim for many years after the Philistines found it to be a threat to their own gods. David wanted it to be restored to its proper place of honor in Israel's worship. After David had subdued his enemies, he moved the Ark respectfully, in the manner prescribed by God, to Jerusalem in preparation for the building of the temple.

What a day! David provided for a celebration by every person in attendance. He cried out before them that they should praise God. He called on all creation, including the Ocean, to praise God. He was ecstatic, and he wanted everyone and everything to join in his ecstasy.

The beauty of creation draws out our praise. It would be hard not to praise God when viewing a sunrise at sea. We think nature motivates our praise. David, however, thought he should motivate nature to give praise. In our world, we think of nature as science, a collection of simple, or not-so-simple, facts. We don't think of it as something with spirit and character. We don't normally think that the ocean or mountains or forests have voices with which to give God praise.

David, a poet and musician, knew better. He recognized that God's creation was full of God's being. It is hard to express the truth that there is more to nature than meets the eye, but there is. If nature were simple mathematics with no spirit, what might it be? Wouldn't everything simply become gray goo over time if there were no guiding spirit? Creation is not a myriad of little gods, nor are trees and rocks imbued with kind or malevolent spirits. Nevertheless, God does give nature a voice, and this is the voice that David calls out. Nature has a voice that always speaks praise. When our busy and stressful world has overwhelmed us and defeated our own spirits, it can be very nourishing to spend time in communion with nature, which always points us to God. The voice of nature is a witness to God's power of creation and the mystery of his love of beauty, not just utility.

Nothing in nature is simply utilitarian. That fact is truly amazing. Look at a dozen pictures of plants and animals and mountain, desert and sea. Notice the variety of ways for a creature to fly. How many different forms can a wave or wavelet take on? Every kind of bird or flower has its own colors and shape. Every little niche in nature is home to some form of life. Nature is not empty or pointless. Nature has a voice, and its voice points us to God.

Paul wrote about this voice:

> The basic reality of God is plain enough. Open your eyes and there it is! By taking a long and thoughtful look at what God has created, people have always been able to see what their eyes as such can't see: eternal power, for instance, and the mystery of his divine being. Romans 1:19 MSG

The voice of nature is always praising God and pointing us to God and reminding us to worship and serve Him. When we engage in our praise, we can invoke nature to join in our praise and thanksgiving just as David did.

I think the first time I really understood this truth was when I saw the place where the lava meets the sea on the island of Hawaii. We hiked across a rugged lava field to reach a place to view this miracle. We had been able to see the plume of steam that rises from this spot long before we even set foot on the lava field. It was hard to walk through the field. Finally we arrived at a place where we could see the fiery red lava flowing into the cold blue ocean. It truly is a point where creation continues. I am not a poet like David, but I found myself singing songs of praise. No one could hear me, because a 20-knot wind was blowing in from the sea. God could hear, of course. In this place, nature pointed me to God. Nature called on me to join its praise and thanksgiving.

When we sail, we love to see new horizons, we seek new adventures, and we discover new truths. No matter where we go in all the earth, we can never escape God's loving, creative presence. In case we are tempted to forget, nature cries out, "Praise the Lord, for his love endures forever!"(Psalm 136:1 NIV)

Day 28

> The earth will be full of the knowledge of the Lord
> as the waters cover the sea.
>
> Isaiah 11:9 NRSV

Hardly a day goes by without a headline about dire events that are predicted for the near future. We are terrorized regularly by people who believe that too many people are fat, too many people drive SUVs, and too many people think democracy is a good thing for the entire world. We are warned about invading bees or rising temperatures or mutating cold viruses. There are plenty of things to be afraid of in the world around us. It is hard to stay positive in the face of the pressure to be afraid.

The Bible gives us a lot of information that fleshes out our perspective on the scary things. Biblical writers consistently remind us that God is with us through disasters and that his perfect plan will triumph over anything humans can do. These writers are not mindless "positive thinkers." They are people who have been through disasters. The Bible is full of famine and racism and abominable malevolence. God's people were starved, enslaved, and abused in every imaginable way. The national leaders of God's chosen people were as phony as any contemporary politician. They regularly sold out the people for personal gain. The Bible does not ever suggest that being one of God's own will guarantee a life of ease and wealth. Rather, the Bible points to a completely different standard of value.

In the Bible, the people who are beloved and valued by God are the poor, the weak, the helpless, the sick, the starving. For their sake, God overturned priestly dynasties and pulled the rug out from under national defense. When challenged, God said that his expectations were simple: "What does the Lord require of you but to do justice, and to love kindness, and to walk humbly with your God?" (Micah 6:8 NRSV)

When Jesus talked about the future, he repeated these values. He described what would come at the end of time, and he repeated the same values: "Whenever you did one of these things to someone overlooked or ignored, that was me" (Matthew 25:40).

Among the common trends in US culture today is a rejection of the notion that Christianity is a national tradition. The diversity of our culture makes it obvious that people find comfort and strength in many religions. If comfort and strength were all Christianity had to offer, it would simply be another club with a supernatural focus.

In Christ, that idea is blown to bits. Jesus Christ was born quietly in a small town in Judea and grew up in the home of a craftsman. He was a descendant of David, the king all Jews revered in memory as the single most important symbol of their nation, but so were a lot of people in the small towns of the Roman provinces within the ancient boundaries of the kingdom of Israel. Very little is known of his childhood, but when he became a man, that changed. He submitted to a baptism of repentance, though he had nothing to repent, and then he embarked on a three-year ministry whose significant teachings recalled the ancient prophesies and built on the most fundamental values spoken of by the prophets.

> You're blessed when you're at the end of your rope. With less of you there is more of God and his rule.
>
> You're blessed when you feel you've lost what is most dear to you. Only then can you be embraced by the One most dear to you.
>
> You're blessed when you're content with just who you are—no more, no less. That's the moment you find yourselves proud owners of everything that can't be bought.
>
> You're blessed when you've worked up a good appetite for God. He's food and drink in the best meal you'll ever eat.
>
> You're blessed when you care. At the moment of being 'care-full,' you find yourselves cared for.
>
> You're blessed when you get your inside world—your mind and heart—put right. Then you can see God in the outside world.
>
> You're blessed when you can show people how to cooperate instead of compete or fight. That's when you discover who you really are, and your place in God's family.
>
> You're blessed when your commitment to God provokes persecution. The persecution drives you even deeper into God's kingdom."
>
> Matthew 5:3-10 MSG

When Jesus left the earth, those who saw him leave looked up into heaven, wondering what they should do next. Angels reminded them that they had work to do, and they promised that Jesus would return, something that should not have been news to them, because Jesus always promised he would be back.

The disciples no doubt recalled Jesus' words about persecution many times in the years to come, as many of his followers would do over the two thousand years between then and now. However, they did not despair. They carried within them the promised Holy Spirit, and they carried a hope for the future that enlightened and enriched their present. Jesus had promised that he would be with them to the end of the world, whenever that should happen, and one by one, they carried their hope to the ends of the earth.

Today it might seem as if the message has surely reached everyone. It is hard to imagine that there is any place that has not heard of Jesus. Moreover, some feel encouraged to predict that the end will be soon. They can just get in line with all the people of eras past who thought they knew when the earth would end.

I don't know when the final cataclysm will come. I don't care. I am happy to live with the hope that Isaiah and Habakkuk found so encouraging and strengthening in times of great despair – the same hope that John described so dramatically in the book of Revelation:

> I saw Heaven and earth new-created. Gone the first Heaven, gone the first earth, gone the sea.
> I saw Holy Jerusalem, new-created, descending resplendent out of Heaven, as ready for God as a bride for her husband.
> I heard a voice thunder from the Throne: "Look! Look! God has moved into the neighborhood, making his home with men and women! They're his people, he's their God. He'll wipe every tear from their eyes. Death is gone for good—tears gone, crying gone, pain gone—all the first order of things gone." The Enthroned continued, "Look! I'm making everything new."
> Revelation 21:1-5 MSG

Day 29

> O Lord, how manifold are your works!
> In wisdom you have made them all;
> the earth is full of your creatures.
> Yonder is the sea, great and wide,
> creeping things innumerable are there,
> living things both small and great.
>
> Psalm 104:24-25 NRSV

The future is dire, if you believe the news. Species are becoming extinct. Coral reefs are dying. The earth is becoming warmer. We are told that in the foreseeable future terrible destruction is coming unless we do something to ward it off. When we accumulate all the warnings and try to make sense of them, we quickly see that fixing one thing has great potential to break another. What is the human race to do? How shall we survive?

This Psalm is a statement of faith in the creator that extends to confidence in his plan for creation. The writer of this Psalm believed that our Creator was so wise that he planned well for all circumstances. The psalmist had confidence in God's wisdom and power to make a world that works, a world that human beings cannot break. He looked at the world around him not in fear, but in awe. He does not scorn learning or analysis, but when he takes in information, he receives it in the context of his faith that God is good, that the creation is good, and that man is not able to thwart God's good purposes.

The Bible says that we are stewards of God's gifts. That is our natural duty as inhabitants of creation. Our obligation of stewardship should incline us to look for opportunities to learn how to live in harmony with creation, and to use the resources of creation wisely and to respect and cherish the beauty of creation. However, the more we study creation, the more we discover how intricately all its elements interact. That discovery should give us great respect for the Creator. It isn't a simple matter at all to change anything in the universal sense. Human beings have not yet mastered the all the elements that are affected by the change of even one variable. It is enough to make someone feel desperate and afraid of disaster.

As we face what looks like impending doom, this psalm should reassure us. God has been managing creation for billions of years. Human beings have been in the picture for only a tiny fraction of that time. Is it even possible that we have had time to learn how to change the world for good or ill – really? This psalm reminds us that God has a plan for creation, and that includes us. We may do things that are not wise, and we should learn to do better. But we need not quail in fear that we can by our actions bring about the end of the world. That cataclysm is in God's hands. All creation is in God's hands. The world may change in dramatic ways, and we may be required to deal with those changes. We may need to do things we haven't yet imagined. However, those changes do not mean that God's plan has failed. The Creator has a plan, and we are part of it.

Day 30

> Then the channels of the sea were seen,
> and the foundations of the world were laid bare
> at your rebuke, O Lord,
> at the blast of the breath of your nostrils.
> He reached down from on high, he took me;
> he drew me out of mighty waters.
> He delivered me from my strong enemy,
> and from those who hated me;
> for they were too mighty for me.
> They confronted me in the day of my calamity;
> but the Lord was my support.
> He brought me out into a broad place;
> he delivered me, because he delighted in me.
>
> Psalm 18:15-19 NRSV

I have started many projects in my life that I did not finish. Every time I have moved, I have taken that occasion as an opportunity to discard projects whose attractions had worn off in midstream. Embroidered napkins. Crocheted doilies. Frilly blouses. I don't always finish what I start.

Thank Goodness, God is not like me. The psalmist here proclaims that when he encountered something he could not manage, God was able to deal with it. God did not start to help him and give up or simply fade away in the middle of the problem. God was so reliable in his life that he felt as if God had reached into the depths of the sea and flipped the waters out of the way in order to rescue him. God stayed with him to the end of his troubles and then gave him a firm place to stand where he could give praise to God his deliverer.

This Psalm is in the list of Psalms attributed to David. If he is the person who wrote it, it is not hard to recall what situations might have inspired it. David faced down Goliath when he was very young, despite the fact that Goliath had intimidated every grown man in the army of Saul. After becoming Saul's darling for a while, David then became *persona non grata* and was pursued by Saul for years, always in danger for his life. David's own sons were rebellious and arrogant, and he had to survive their uprisings, even going into exile. David's life was not easy. Yet in this Psalm, as in many others, he acknowledges that no matter how bleak his future looked at any moment, he was never alone. He had the experience of being rescued over and over by God, who could not be defeated by anything. David's relationship with God sustained him in times of trouble. By faith, he placed himself in God's hands. He recognized that he was not a self-made man; he was a God-made man.

David had a lot of goals and aspirations as king of Israel. He didn't achieve all of them. He learned that some of his objectives were not God's objectives, and he had to accept punishment when he went down the wrong road. He learned that he might fail God, but God never failed him.

God is not a magician who hears our prayers and grants our wishes. We cannot manipulate God, but we can trust him. In our darkest hours, when we have turned away or gotten lost or forgotten our priorities, we can call to him and he will hear. He said that he would be with us always. We can count on God to finish what he starts.

Day 31

> Comfort, O comfort my people,
> says your God.
> Speak tenderly to Jerusalem,
> and cry to her
> that she has served her term,
> that her penalty is paid,
> that she has received from the Lord's hand
> double for all her sins
>
> Isaiah 40:1-2 NRSV

Do you know how it feels to receive double punishment for all your sins? I think I do. On the one hand, I know that I have deserved every punishment I ever received, but on the other hand I look around at some people who I think deserve even more, yet they appear to skate through life unscathed. I have probably not literally received double for my sins, but at times I have certainly felt that way.

Of course, Jerusalem didn't literally receive double, either. After all, anyone who cares a whit for the truth could see in the story of the children of Israel that they were never at any time faithful to their covenant with God. Double? From some point of view, it might seem that they had never really been punished. After all, didn't God come to their rescue every single time that they cried out and said they were sorry? The fact that God finally sent them away in exile from Jerusalem and let some foreign heathen populate the holy city with aliens was trivial when compared to the centuries during which they played games with him, trying to make him believe they were faithful because they showed up for his festivals, even though they much more loved the fertility rites for the idols of their neighbors. I don't have much trouble realizing that God felt betrayed and scorned by such a breach of faith.

I have no trouble realizing that I deserve the same. Many times have I read Jesus' words, "Love your enemy. Do good to those who hurt you" (Matthew 5:44 NET), yet I still look for ways to give back to my enemy what I have received. I have read the words that say that what I do "for the least of these," I do to Jesus, and I sort of forget that those words apply whether I am doing good or ill to the "least of these." Looking at my deeds by that standard, I know that I have caused Jesus great pain. I already deserve real punishment I have not yet received.

Isaiah gives me hope, as he gave hope to the exiled inhabitants of Jerusalem. No matter what I have done, no matter what I deserved, no matter what has happened to me, I am not forgotten. God still loves me. All this punishment broke his heart, and now he is going to come for me.

When I was about eight years old, my brother and I got into a bad habit. My parents had received a five-pound box of shelled pecans as a Christmas present, and my mother kept it in the refrigerator. My brother and I loved those nuts. At first we only sneaked a couple of pieces every once in a while, but the flavor was delicious and the temptation was great. Eventually, we were dipping out a handful almost every day after school if mother were not in the house. Needless to say, it became evident at some point that the nuts were disappearing. The day came when we faced our punishment.

It was an era before spanking became unfashionable. As the eldest, I was first. I bent over Mother's sewing bench. She took her brush in hand and administered the spanking. I cried. Then I stood up and turned around. Mother was crying, too. "Being a mother means you must do hard things," she said. "What you did hurt our family, and what I had to do hurt me." We put our arms around each other and cried together. Years later, facing the infractions of my own children, I learned what that moment was all about.

I think it is like that for God. I know it was like that with Israel. Over and over in the Bible, God calls out to Israel, "Come back, come back." When he cries out to Israel, he is crying out to the whole human race, "Come back, come back." He punishes people who have scorned and dishonored him, but all the while he is weeping for the broken fellowship. In Isaiah 40, he says that having punished sinners as they deserve, he will do more than allow them to return; he will permanently mend what is broken. Rather than impose any more punishment on those he loves, he will take care of the problem permanently. He will take the punishment himself.

It makes you ask, why would he do this? To whom is he accountable that he should do this? Isaiah asks, too.

> Who has measured the waters in the hollow of his hand
> and marked off the heavens with a span,
> enclosed the dust of the earth in a measure,
> and weighed the mountains in scales
> and the hills in a balance?
> Who has directed the spirit of the Lord,
> or as his counselor has instructed him?
> Whom did he consult for his enlightenment,

> and who taught him the path of justice?
> Who taught him knowledge,
> and showed him the way of understanding?
> Even the nations are like a drop from a bucket,
> and are accounted as dust on the scales;
> see, he takes up the isles like fine dust.
> Lebanon would not provide fuel enough,
> nor are its animals enough for a burnt offering.
> All the nations are as nothing before him;
> they are accounted by him as less than nothing and emptiness.
> To whom then will you liken God,
> or what likeness compare with him?
>
> Isaiah 40:12-18 NRSV

The answer is that God is accountable to no one. He doesn't owe anyone anything. Nobody taught him. Nobody directed him. The forces of nature and the power of nations are nothing compared to him. Yet he leans down from heaven to touch us and heal us and take on himself the punishment we deserve.

It shouldn't be a surprise. When God made his covenant with Abraham, that is what he promised. Abraham stood by and watched God agree to take on the bloody fate of the torn animals of the covenant, and Abraham took on nothing. God made a promise, and Abraham was the recipient. When God said through Isaiah that he would comfort Jerusalem, the way my mother hugged me after my spanking, he was remaining faithful to his promise from the beginning. When he walked through Jerusalem with his cross and died the punishing, shameful death of crucifixion, he remained faithful to his eternal promise.

We all know that we deserve punishment, but we hate to acknowledge that truth. God hates it too, and that is why he took it for us. The punishment has been meted out, and Jesus is the one who took it for us. What a comfort it is, to turn toward Jesus in our tears and see that he is also weeping, spreading his arms out in love to welcome us home.

Afterword

Writing this book was a labor of love – love of the ocean, joy in Christ, and gratefulness for wonderful Christians in Omaha and Baltimore who helped me to grow in faith.

If you enjoyed this book, you might enjoy reading my blog at http://livingontilt.com. You are also invited to write to katherine@katherineharms.com with any thoughts you care to share.

Notes

1 Leovy as quoted at
http://potw.news.yahoo.com/s/potw/49321/the-invisible-war?start_row=1131

2 Junger, Sebastian, The Perfect Storm (W. W. Norton and Company © 1997) p. 138

3 Henry, Matthew: Matthew Henry's Commentary on the Whole Bible : Complete and Unabridged in One Volume. Peabody : Hendrickson, 1996, c1991, S. Ps 89:5

Made in the USA
Columbia, SC
23 January 2019